Time Well Spent

Jenna Cohen

A COLLECTION OF POETRY, SONGS, AND SHORT ESSAYS

jennacohencreations.com

Time Well Spent by Jenna Cohen

Published by JDW Press

1153 Garson Ave., Rochester, NY 14609

www.jennacohencreations.com

Cover by Jenna Cohen.

Canva, Online Design and Publishing Tool

ISBN: 9781735190112 (ebook)

Dedication

For my Mommala who loves me fiercely, nourishes my spirit, and made me who I am. I love you more.

~ Your Sweetness ~

Table of Contents

Poetry.......7

They Say It Takes a Village.......8
The Way I See You.......10
Wanderer.......12
What Truly Matters.......14
Awakening Grace.......20
Unconditional.......21
Goodbye.......22
Where Terror Reigns.......26
Affirmations.......27
I Plant Flowers in Potholes.......28
Lost and Unfound.......30
Time Well Spent.......32
Selfless Prayers.......33
Life in the Lap Lane.......36
I Feel Fire (poem).......38
To the People Who Look Like Me.......40

Songs.......43

Diamond.......44
Let Freedom Ring.......45
Last Dance.......48
I Am Brave.......50
I Feel Fire (song).......52
You Should Be So Lucky.......53
Love Completely.......56
Ally's Lullaby.......57

Table of Contents

Short Essays....................................59

Heart of a Teacher, Soul of a Mensch....................................60
Why We Come to Church....................................62
Puzzle Piece....................................64
Procedure Day....................................66
The Class of 2012....................................71
The Unspoken....................................73
Hand-Me-Down Legacy....................................80

About the Author....................................85

Acknowledgements....................................86

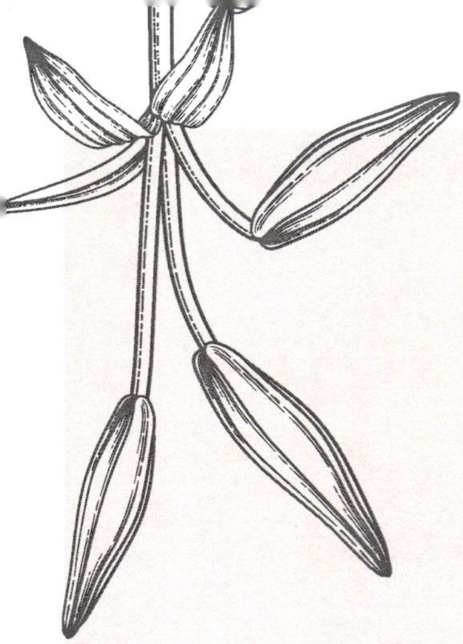

POETRY

They Say it Takes a Village

They say it takes a village
But for me it took a miracle
You see because life didn't just give me lemons
It's gave me brick wall barriers
Mortar and stone
Deep angry oceans
And fire

They say it takes a village
And a village it took indeed

For my village looked like families bonded not just by blood but by destiny
It looked like parents of friends who made their houses home to me when mine became unsafe
It looked like teachers expanding my mind
Who taught me to think critically and to speak with intention
Who provided me with creative outlets
And graced my life with kindness and compassion
It looked like healthcare professionals
Who gave me answers and treated me with patience and dignity
It looked like a faith community who reminded me of the goodness in humanity
Who taught me to question and wonder
Who held me together and bandaged the broken pieces of myself
Who taught me to lead with an open heart and to listen with an open mind

They say it takes a village
But what they mean is that this world will give you insurmountable obstacles
That you will build an amour out of scar tissue
And scaffolding to help you stand tall
But the world will also give you people to hold you up
So that even when adversity comes, you have hands to help you carry the weight of the world that rests on your shoulders
Human progress is made when those unite in difference

The woman that stands before you did not always exist
She was built from the ground up
It was my village that helped me love myself
That guided me during times of trial
Who instilled in me great ambition
And fierce determination to match
My village gave me confidence
And taught me that no dream is too big and no star is too far out of reach

They say it takes a village
And my village saved my life

The Way I See You

One of my favorite sounds is your laugh
Not the one that hides your darkness and tucks away anger, concealing emotions from even yourself
Not the laugh that shields your heart from hurt and placates to others for protection
But the one that sneaks up on you when you least expect it
The one that greets you as an old friend, welcoming you home
The one that catches you off guard
And if you're still
And looking very closely
It catches that twinkle in your eye
That sound replays in my mind and holds a piece of my heart

The man I met all those years ago stands before me unhinged from burden
No longer lost in anguish
Actively blossoming in front of me
The thing about Spring that is too often overlooked is the time it takes for regrowth

Seasons change before we feel it in our bones
Soil absorbs melting snow
Birds return from their adventure South
Small budding appears, dancing in the crisp breeze

Your soul fosters an internal Spring
Shedding layers of scar tissue you built as armor to survive
Despite the roots of your tree being worn and unattended
You grow
You rise
You yearn for more, eager to take life by its horns
Proclaiming loudly the happiness you deserve

And on the days where clouds roll in, fading the light within you
The wind may howl, the flowers may wilt
And fear might start to creep in
Remind the mirror that you are a work of art
Forged into a diamond from insurmountable pressure
Look to the sky
Breathe in fresh air
Take a step forward
And remember the way I see you

Wanderer

I've spent my days restlessly scouring the earth
for a place of safety
A sanctuary to exhale the woes I carry
Sleepless nights I've searched my dreams
Rings of darkness hang from under my eyes
Rippling
Will I ever find a bed that's not too hard or not
too soft to rest my golden locks
A place that fits
Just right

My need for kinship has taken me to some
unexpected places
On unexpected adventures
With unexpected people
Curious
Interesting
I went looking for affirmation from every soul I
came upon
Attaching myself to people and places in which I
did not belong
Finding myself discontent
Without comfort
In need of warmth

The search continues
The balls of my feet propel me forward
Quickening
Eager to discover whatever comes next

Is there a corner of this world just for me
Tailor-made to call my own
My home
But where is home for a wandering soul
Lost
Looking for acceptance wherever she roams
A chameleon disguised in human form
Shapeshifting to fit the mold she mistakes for identity
Outside my body, looking in
Examining my own humanity
Where have you been, old friend?

What Truly Matters

Dear 18-year-old me
I'm sorry
I'm sorry this world failed to teach you what truly matters
Before it was too late
I'm sorry you never learned to love and respect yourself
To treat your body like the temple it is and to embrace your curves
I'm sorry that the world taught you that having big breasts was an invitation for men to comment on them

And while we're on apologies
I'm sorry health class did teach you that having an orgasm is what matters most about sex
I'm sorry health class failed to teach you the definitions of coercion and consent
Because consent IS in fact what matters most when it comes to sex
I'm sorry the world taught you that what you wear "implies" consent

It DOES NOT matter what you wear
And it didn't matter what you wore that night
It didn't matter the decisions you made leading up to it
Or the things you consented to previously
It didn't matter that you met in math class and he seemed like a nice guy
Because it turns out it didn't matter that you said no
It didn't matter that you said no A LOT of times before he took what he wanted anyway
It didn't matter that he felt bad afterwards and apologized for his "mistake"
Because nothing he could do or say could take back what he had already stolen
And that DOES matter
It matters that after fleeing for safety from that place every breath you took felt thicker
It matters that the first thing you heard after escaping his apartment was the cat call of another man ogling your body
I guess there really is no escape after all, is there

It mattered that the male cop you told what happened looked
disgusted because that validated that what happened to you
was wrong
It matters that the female detective who showed up to your
apartment unannounced the next day blamed you for what
happened
That you were too young and naïve to understand.
It didn't matter that your jaw was sore and swollen from his
use of force
Or that you said no
Or that you fought back
That didn't stop her from asking you if your attacker had a
big penis
And when you timidly choked out "yes" she said, "Well maybe
that's what guys with big penises think blowjobs are supposed
to be like"
WELL FUCK THAT LADY BECAUSE SHE WAS WRONG!
And THAT matters

Dear Dad
I'm sorry
And thank you
Thank you for being the person I could call to come pick me up
Thank you for making me go to the hospital when I didn't want to
Thank you for holding my hand
For staying with me when they asked their questions and ran their tests
Thank you for letting me know that you were there for me and for proving it with your actions
Thank you for not blaming me when that's all I could do
Thank you for showing me that not every man wants to hurt me
Thank you
I love you

Dear present-day me
Congratulations
I am so proud of you
You survived and continue to survive and thrive every day, in spite of

You are a strong, independent, and fierce woman
You have kindness, compassion, and a deep love for others rooted in your bones
And you refused to let him take that away from you
You are a fucking super hero
And you matter
Do you understand me
YOU matter
I know that you're scared
You fear that your younger cousins will suffer the same fate
That others you love will become another statistic, as you have
But what matters is that they have you
Yes, people who hear your story may look at you differently
But that doesn't matter
What matters is that they will understand you better
Your sensitivity
Your passion for activism
Your eagerness to advocate for and to raise the voices of others

You have surrounded yourself with people who love you
unconditionally
Who accept you for who you are
And THAT matters
It's a fortunate thing to know that you are loved
And you are
Oh so very much
And those that hold you in their hearts- they matter
And you deserve one another

Dear attacker
I'm sorry
I'm sorry this world failed to teach you what truly matters
Before it was too late

Awakening Grace

Life is about finding emotion
Wearing a smile in depths of darkness
Living with pain and seeking devotion
Discovering love and the joys of bliss
God, grant me the serenity of change,
The strength to fight and power to forgive
All that lies beneath me must rearrange
So I'll lead the life I was meant to live
I hear angels sing messages of peace
A soft melody that cradles the ear
I have awakened and let pain release
So angst and strife have no bounds to exist
I've opened my eyes to a brand new place
Where I've found love and the meaning of grace

Unconditional

If only there was a word that went beyond "love"
There is no singular phrase that measures all that you are in my heart
No word to express how every glimmer of light captures the twinkle in your eye
Or how the crackle of your laughter echoes in every flame you spin
For ours, my friend, is the only love story that matters
What started out as a choice
Grew to be destiny
Our souls are bound to one another

Your love has taught me to endure
Every breath I take is one in which you have saved
Every tomorrow I awake is one in which you have lead me to
I carry you with me in every funny story
With every smile
Every rough day
Or piece of good news
You are my person
Even on your worst of days when your strength grows weary
And your light falls dim
Your need for assurance is my call to action
Fear not kindred spirit
You will never walk this earth alone
Here I am

Goodbye

Big brother
I miss you
I wish I remembered your warm embrace
But I've only seen it in photos.
A little toe-headed boy
Arms wrapped around his baby sister's cradle
Protecting her from the world around her
Snap shots of a life I never knew
I used to imagine what it'd be like to know your gentleness
To not feel fear when you entered a room
Heart racing
Or heard your voice
Hands shaking
Or spoke your name
Eyes welling with tears

Something within you has always been haunted
And your misery certainly loved my company
Tried as I might, I couldn't save you
I long for the presence of a ghost.
A shell of a man I barely know

Growing up in close quarters didn't bring us together
You were always far away
Until you weren't

Heart racing
Until you got angry
Hands shaking
Until mama and papa weren't around
Eyes welling with tears

When did you start to hate me?
Before or after you'd throw your first blow
Heart racing
Before or after you'd drag me by my hair
Hands shaking
Before or after you'd tell me I'm worthless
Eyes welling with tears

Hide behind the garage in the dirt
Build a garden so you feel safe
Collect fossils to escape to a different time
A different place
Any other place but this

Holes in the walls
Echoes in our hearts
A broken family
All suffering from your abuse
But when does bad behavior become a choice and not a product of mental illness?
13?
18?
30?
Never?

Your claims of love rang empty
Love doesn't come with bruises or swollen lips
Heart racing
Or night terrors
Hands shaking
Or threats
Eyes welling with tears
You don't hide from love on a shelf in the closet praying it doesn't find you

Hide under the stairwell
Build a fort and call it a game
Practice holding your breath so he can't hear you
Sing songs in your head to find remnants of peace

I still wake in your shadows at night
Haunted by memories I thought I had buried in that garden on Matthews Street
I planted flowers in the potholes your storm left behind
Softening the cracked and jagged pieces inside me

I had to give up the potential future of us together, happy
It's hard to mourn a man who still walks the earth
I'm so sorry
I had to give you up
I am no longer willing to sacrifice my sanity just so you don't walk alone in a darkness of your own creation
I worked too hard to be happy
I will no longer be your punching bag

The woman I am I built from the ground up
She is rooted in strength
No longer slave to your anguish
I choose freedom
I choose joy
I choose safety
I choose myself
I am the master of my destiny
You don't control me anymore

I grieve an existence that will never be
I pray you find happiness and peace in your life
I look forward to a future where the thought of you is not so painful
Goodbye big brother
Maybe we'll get it right in the next life

Where Terror Reigns

When you don't know who you are, you fall prey to the
falsehoods others accuse you to be
Ugly untruths will lay claim to a throne that is abdicated
There is no justice in the words and deeds of men who
possess no nobility
Though his convictions may be strong, let yours be stronger
Concede nothing

If there is nothing else guaranteed in this world
Let it be this
Only you hold the depth to your own majesty
Declare your rule with veracity
Hold your integrity with fists tightly clenched
A kingdom where terror reigns is a kingdom unruled
So turn your rust into gold
Lavish yourself with jewels
The finest of silks with ornate figures
And pretty things
With pretty words
And goodness in abundance

Pick up your crown, Queen
Terror's reign ends today.

Affirmations

Good enough
Good?
Enough?
Enough!
I'm tired of trying to prove my worth
I've proven it by existing
I matter?
Matter
The atoms and particles that make up the very fabric of my being
The neurons that fire from my brain throughout my body
The blood coursing through my veins
I was HERE
My matter matters

Bury me in the earth
Let my body become one with the soil that grips the trees, keeping them rooted as they grow strong
Branching out into the world
Leaves outstretched as if to embrace the wind
Let my soul become another ring of bark wrapped around the tree's trunk
Let it exhale oxygen into the air
Creating breath
Creating life
Contributing to the world long after I am gone
I am not gone
I am HERE
I am good
I am enough
I matter

I Plant Flowers In Potholes

You are the strongest person I know
But your soul is cloaked in darkness
Another person, hardly a man
Who lashes out
Who seeks control
You taught me that anger was a monster
Living in the bellows of your soul
With sharp hateful words
Who uses violence to scare those around him into obeying his beck and call
You see because the monster is greedy
He keeps you held captive in his rage
And only lets you out when it's time to apologize for his mistakes

They ask me why I stay
Why if I miss your call I'm terrified
Because even if you scream and shout
At least I know that you're alive
I tried to be your savior
But it nearly cost me my own life
Save mama
Save papa
Bury the pain way down inside

Trick them with my humor
Fool them with my smarts
But if you looked beneath my smile
You'd see I was falling apart
Beaten and tattered
A hollow shell behind my eyes
I had to learn to mend my wounds
Because I was determined to survive
I learned to create magic
To see the beauty in the broken
And despite all that we have struggled
For you, my heart remains open
I plant flowers in potholes
I find renewal and rebirth in what appears to be concrete
I live
And thrive
And grow
And learn
There's nothing within me that knows defeat

Lost and Unfound

My muscles ache from all these circles I'm
running 'round
Missing pieces of my body
Distorted
Discarded
Never found

Doctors pass the buck until you're too tired to
seek more answers
Leaving you questioning and wondering if this
was your own failure

Wasn't I good?
Wasn't I kind?
Why was this chosen as my path
I've journeyed
I've suffered
Seen through the looking glass

Poor Mama
Poor Papa
Watchful eyes have seen how they've
sacrificed

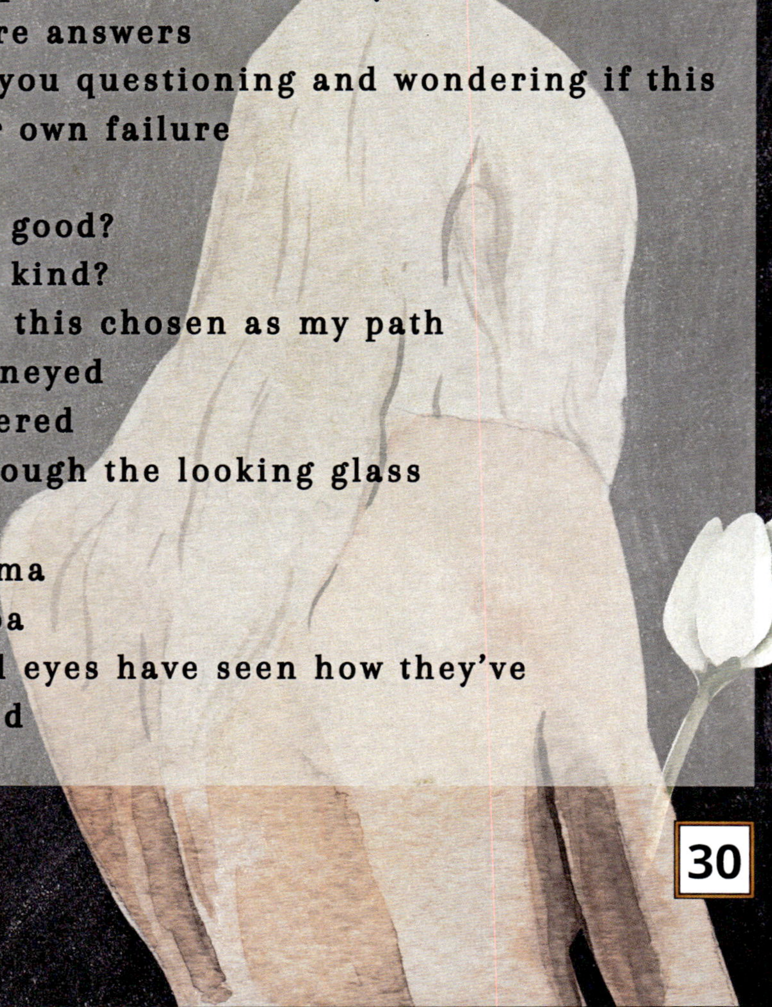

Their hands clasped together begging God
"Please, any relief will suffice"
Bloodshot eyes have laid awake
Unable to answer their child's helpless cries
Forehead kisses
Bedtime stories
Can't heal pain with lullabies

This has been an exhaustive existence
Is desiring normality so very wrong
I sit here fighting off my demons with
thoughtful poems and pretty songs
The pain isn't just in my body
It's a riddle that toys with my mind
Is this normal?
Is this real?
Am I disabled enough this time?
I'm tired of second-guessing
Too drained to feel confusion
Oh, how I long for this to have always been an
illusion

Time Well Spent

Darkness surrounds me now
Eclipsing the light inside me that's always seemed to shine so bright
It's seeped in through the cracked and jagged pieces of myself I thought I had so carefully tended to
Bandaids all the same, it seems
I've written of triumph
Of love
Of endurance
Of strength
But strength has such an ugly sound to me now
Strength is what I told myself I saw in the mirror
Feeble efforts to convince myself to keep on living
Pain is the darkness that holds my soul captive
The dragon hoarding it's queen who's locked away in a tower so close to the heavens
She can observe the beauty of the world
The subjects she influences
Enjoy the feeling of the sun when she steps outside her window, looking down

If I were to fall from this tower
Wouldn't the grass feel like freedom when I reach the ground?

Selfless Prayers

God- guide my Brother
Help him find joy and fill the empty pieces in
his life
Give him the freedom to search
Search for himself
Whoever that person may be
Shoulder him from the cruelness of the world
For he has suffered enough
Protect him from those that try to tear him
down
Even if that person may be himself
God- please save my Brother
Save him from himself

God- guide my Mother
Show her the true beauty that lies within
herself
Restore the broken fragments of her dignity
and self-esteem
For she is the essence of love
Teach her to shed that love upon herself before
all others
And not to apologize for mistakes she might
have made
We are only human
God- please save my Mother
Save her from herself

God- guide my Father
Reassure him of his surrounding light
For I fear that he has lost his way
Teach him to focus less on the materialistic
environment he surrounds himself with
And instead focus on his health
Steer him in the direction of strength
Encourage him to overcome temptation
God- please save my Father
Save him from himself

God- guide my Sister
Support her on the path she chooses to take in
life
For it is her life to live and not that of those
around her
Open the doors of opportunity and courage
Courage to strive for opportunities that she has
let pass by
Lift her when she feels she has no one
For I may not always be there to catch the tears
that fall
May the world show her kindness and
compassion
Compassion she has never failed to give freely
God- please save my Sister
Save her from herself

God- guide Me
Open up your golden gates and free me of the burden I've had to carry
Bring me peace of mind that I have done something right
Give me a sign that I am not alone
Forgive me
For I have been selfish
I ask you to help my Brother- when I am the one who feels at need
I ask you to show my Mother- when I am the one who feels unworthy
I ask you to reassure my Father- when I am the one who has lost my way
I ask you to support my sister- when I am the one in need of compassion
Forgive me God
I have lied in the name of selfless intentions
I am the one who needs guidance
God- please save Me
Save me from myself

Life in the Lap Lane

My mind is the loudest room to occupy
Vivid
Chaotic
Confined
Radiating heat through my synapses
Imagination rapidly expanding
Piles of paperwork and unwritten notes await me in the morning
Greeting me with a crooked smile
Taunting
Thoughts compound and multiply
Until I submerge
Breathe 1,2,3
Breathe 1,2,3
Lofty urges to swim the English Channel
Followed by internal criticism
Instructing me to be realistic in my daydreaming
Withholding permission to have passerby desires
Compromised
Muffled
Cold
Breathe 1,2,3
Breathe 1,2,3
The chaos focuses
Streamlined
Almost meditative
Sweet relief
Breathe 1 2 3
Breathe 1 2 3

Images of hills from childhood camps
Summer's misty morning dew
Holidays spent with family
The feeling of water as I glide through
Breathe 1 2 3
Breathe 1 2 3
Fragments of poetry trickle in
Fantastical storytelling conceived from creativity
Book signings
Speaking engagements
Talk shows eager to hear about my inspiration
Breathe
1
2
3
Breathe
1
2
3
I emerge
Momentary quiet while I catch my breath
Quick expanses of my chest
Heart racing
Wave to the lifeguard as if to thank her for bearing
witness to my momentary tranquility
See you on Thursday

I Feel Fire

It's like flames
Burning inside, scratching their way toward the surface but remaining hidden from view
It's like pain
Underlying or overwhelming for no reason at all
Or for reasons that shouldn't have consequences
It's like people telling you if only you lost this much weight
Or took this medication
Or tried this exercise
Or saw this doctor
Maybe then you'd be happy
Or at least satisfied
It's like feeling selfish for wanting to be able to walk everyday

It's like feeling you're a constant burden
And fearing the unknown
For what is to become of the girl who's unknowns are waking up and needing help putting on clothes
Or going to the bathroom
Or carrying her things
Or cooking her meal
Or driving her to the hospital
It's like when sick days don't apply to you because they don't make days for pain
It's like rationing your medication because your insurance ran out
Or won't cover the meds you need
Or wants you to defend why you need them
Even though you've been on them for years

And have a diagnosis
And a prescription from your doctor
And prior authorization
It's like the gray areas are all you exist in
Or reading between the lines to find your name
It's like being too poor to afford the care you need
But not being healthy enough to earn the wealth you need to acquire it
I feel fire
Lit from within
My soul ablaze
It's like being trapped in a body that doesn't match your fierce determination
Your passion
Your drive
It's like remembering you were once capable of so much more
And longing for the days of the past
It's like fighting an invisible war that strangers have a lot of opinions about
And not being disabled enough
I feel fire
But no one can see me burn

To the People Who Look Like Me

To the people who look like me

It's time for us to sit down and have a little conversation
I ask you to listen openly and exercise healthy confrontation

For what is patriotism if not fighting for what is right
But instead we debate semantics than acknowledge our privilege because we're white
No one is taking away the struggles you've faced
Only asking you accept that there are some struggles in which our color doesn't embrace
Rather than get defensive, digging your heels in the sand
All too often we turn our cheeks instead of reaching out a hand

But what is our responsibility you ask?
We have a duty to learn from our past
To do that we must listen to those who differ from us
Trust their truth
However ugly
However unjust

Looking away from the truth is an act of violence
Progress has never been made when those who witnessed suffering stayed silent

And Mr. Officer as you sit there feeling protected by your vest
Mothers are on their knees begging God their sons have bulletproof chests

And this experience is one that you and I may empathize
But for us to sit here and say we know that fear would be nothing short of lies

To the people who look like me standing by idol
Saying, but what do I do?

Raise your voice up so they can shout a little less
But make sure your information is correct
Speaking loudly without a message does not have an effect
Focus on the impact of your actions rather than your intent
For even actions in the name of love can cause harm that was not meant
When you disrespect your values you disrespect yourself
And if you don't have respect for you
How can you for someone else?

SONGS

Diamond

I'm bright and shiny to people all around me
But they can't see inside
I'm hurt and angry
And frankly it amazed me
They fell for this disguise

I'm bright and shiny to people all around me
But they can't see inside
They poke and praise me
And try to imitate me
And I feel like a fraud

Let Freedom Ring

I bow my head down to pray
Who will guide the way
With hate on the rise
I see fear in the eyes
Oh my brothers and sisters I beg
Hold your fist to the sky
We must stand and fight
Cause the past has evolved, it's still alive

Hear the people say

For a nation United
We sure are Divided
Walls don't protect our liberty
Hate won't destroy us
If we lift our voices
Together in solidarity
Let freedom ring

I don't wanna be here
Tired of feeling so scared
How many more must we lose 'til somebody cares
March streets screaming their names
Wielding privilege and pain
Demanding some justice and radical change

Hear the people say

For a nation United
We sure are Divided
Walls don't protect our liberty
Hate won't destroy us
If we lift our voices
Together in solidarity
Let freedom ring

An invisible war
Feels we've been here before
Generations enslaved
Caged until present day
Time to clean up the mess that we
have made

For a nation United
We sure are Divided
Walls don't protect our liberty
Hate won't destroy us
If we lift our voices
Together in solidarity

Let freedom ring

Last Dance

On your shoulders, I grew older
Playing song and dance
Lift me higher, I was guided
Giving me the chance

To soar
To glide
To reach all new heights
You showed me how to be loved
To laugh
To smile
You held me for a while
When I look back, how time has passed

And I believe you empowered me
You gave me wings to fly
Embrace your flaws
Keep your head up and stand tall
Be proud of who you are

Your example, I will follow
You raised me to be strong
Our new found distance
Tests our limits
Our love, it carries on

The tears
We've cried
And all we've sacrificed
But together we always got through
And you
I know
Will always guide me home
You taught me how to love myself

And I believe you empowered me
You gave me wings to fly
Embrace your flaws
Keep your head up and stand tall
Be proud of who you are

I take
Your hand
Inviting you to stand
Won't you save me this last dance

I Am Brave

Beautiful brown eyed girl
Since when did the weight of the world
Rest on your shoulders, while nobody noticed
Yeah I see the pain in your eyes
From the deception and the lies
Nobody bothered to compromise because they weren't there
'Cause they didn't care

But I've seen those golden gates
And I thought I'd met my fate
I gave it all I could take
But they weren't there
And God was too late
But I am brave

Now is the time to hold on
Just pick your head up and stay strong
And if you're nervous, I can assure this
You're not alone in this fight
Don't hide behind internal night
There's a difference in wrong and right
And if you're scared
And if life isn't fair
I will be there

Cause I've seen those golden gates
And I thought I'd met my fate
I gave it all I could take
But they weren't there
And God was too late
But I am brave

Oh you make life worthwhile
And if the world you think is jaded
And your heart you feel is breaking
Just look in the mirror and say
I am brave

'Cause I've seen those golden gates
And I thought I met your fate
I gave it all I could take
But they weren't there
And God was too late
But I are brave

I Feel Fire

I feel fire, deep inside
But no one can see these flames
burning bright
Trapped in a body, a prison, a cell
Invisible me reaching out for some help
But I won't let go
No I'm holding on
And I won't give up
'Cause I was built strong

Oh and when the waves crash down
Oh you won't see me drown
And my roots keep me grounded
I branch out toward the sky
And these broken wings finally learned how to fly
Oh I will leave my mark
'Cause the fire finally turned into a spark
I was born to survive

You Should Be So Lucky

How does time stand still
Yet seem so far away
As my heart endures
Memories can't seem to stay

Laughter echoes through the house
Familiar sounds I know
I have sat here long ago
My kids have grown their own

A Brooklyn girl
Who's now seen the world
Who's hands have seemed to age

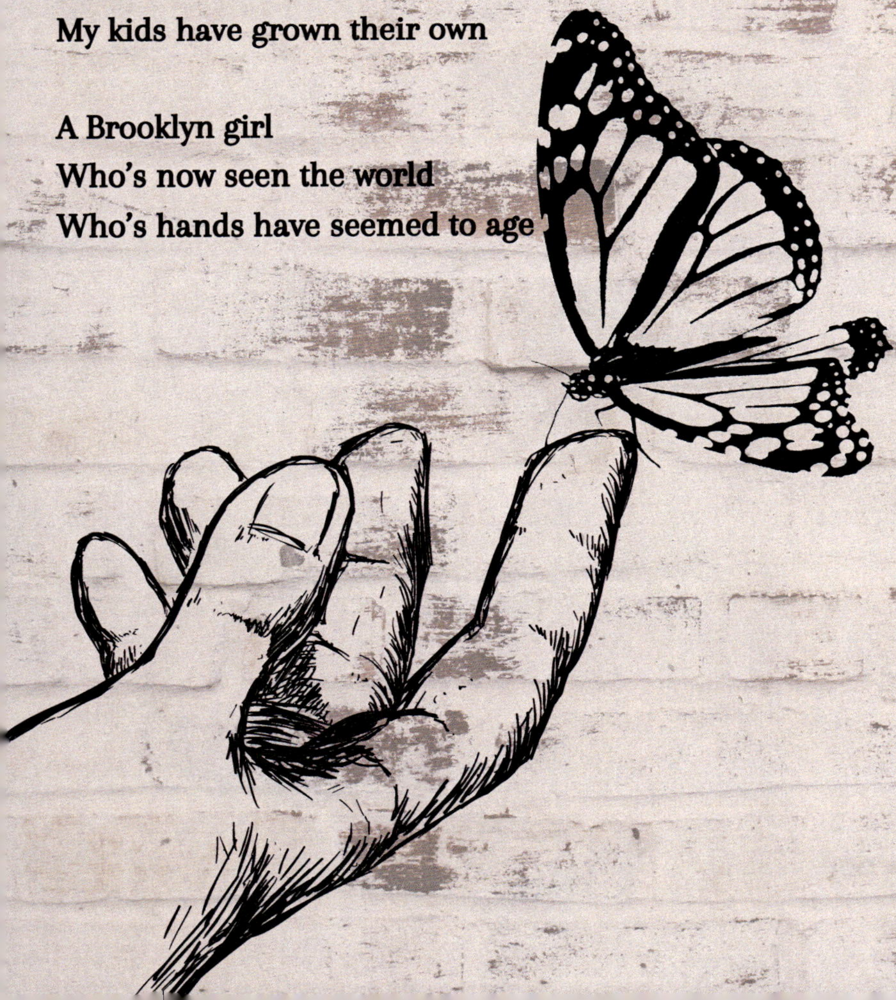

Do the best you can with what you've got
Your differences set you apart
I may not have the best memory
But confidence is all you need
Let my love be my legacy
You should be so lucky

All those years ago
My body bore four children
Now I lay eyes on you
My wonderful grandchildren

Everyone comes with a full
Package that we carry
All that life has brought us through
The challenges did vary

A Brooklyn girl
Who's now seen the world
Not lost my sense of humor

Do the best you can with what you've got
Your differences set you apart
I may not have the best memory
But confidence is all you need
Let my love be my legacy
You should be so lucky

I never want to look back on my life and say
I coulda, I shoulda, I woulda done differently

And let my love be my legacy
You should be so lucky

Love Completely

Children playing in the sunshine
Their laughter makes my heart smile
And I go back
Scenes of the past
Replaying in my mind

Early days were filled with anger
My reflection is a stranger
I was afraid
Pain filled my days
A life forever changed

Maybe the world around me's breaking
Circumstance is changing
But I refuse to come back now that I'm high off the ground
Days seem as if time is so fleeting
I know how you're feeling we're at war within ourselves.

Learning, to love myself completely
The weary and the empty are parts of me that courage pushes 'til the walls come down
At last, simpler days have come back
Cherishing the gift of life we've yet to figure out.

I wanna skip ahead when all reveals itself

Ally's Lullaby

Goodnight Ally
I love you
If you're hurt, I'll heal you
If you're sad, I'll dry all your tears
And soon all your troubles will disappear

Float away on a soft white cloud
Sleep tight, soft and sound
Rest your head on your pillow
Watch the clouds through your window
Close your eyes and fall asleep
If you want I'll start to count sheep

So goodnight Ally
I love you
If you're hurt, I'll heal you
If you're sad, I'll dry all your tears
And soon all your troubles will disappear

SHORT ESSAYS

Heart of a Teacher, Soul of a Mensch

How do you sum up the life of a titan? A person of such integrity and influence, power and purpose. How do you package that neatly into a box and return it to the earth? I don't know how to say goodbye to you, Grandpa. So instead, I'll kiss you on your proverbial keppela and say, "Take care of yourself, you hear?"

I've been asking myself lately how to honor your memory and the best answer I could come up with was to take the lessons you taught me and continue to share them with the world, as you intended. I present: The Martin J. Cohen Lesson Plan of Life.

The learning objectives for the students of this course are as follows:

1. To know the importance of family and heritage.
2. Take pride in who you are and where you come from. This family was born with resilience and strength coursing through our blood. We are the most important thing we will ever have. There is nothing we cannot overcome together. Cherish each other.

3. Knowing history is essential for making progress.
4. Stand up for what is right unapologetically.
5. Find appreciation, peace, and contentment in the natural world around you.
6. Laughter is the greatest medicine.
7. True wealth in life does not come from financial means but rather an abundance of love.
8. Happiness and success are measured differently for everyone. Live a purposeful life and happiness and success will soon come.
9. Your mark on the world matters. You are not just a ripple in the water, you are a wave in ocean. Pushing and pulling, swelling and crashing, constantly moving and changing. Persistent and stubborn; Part of something much greater than you will ever know.

Grandpa, you were no ordinary man. You were the mentor and role model to so many, including myself. My heart will always feel a little empty without you here. Your physical presence may be gone, but your profound mark on the world will forever be felt and carried on by those you loved and those who loved you.

Why We Come to Church

When I was 10, I became physically disabled. Now you may say, but Jenna I've seen you up and moving around- you don't look disabled. Yes, thank you, I've worked very hard on that. Sometimes you may see me using my wheelchair or walking with a little less pep to my step. But most of the time, I walk the earth with an invisible pain unseen by the eye. I'm sure many among us can understand that feeling.

A couple years ago one of my friends started having significant health problems and was in the process of being diagnosed. She called me to come over because as a person who has lived with chronic illness, she knew I would understand. While she, her boyfriend, and I sat on the couch catching up, my friend realized that a lot of the people in her life struggle with chronic illness and disability. Suddenly, she discovered she was joining a club she never signed up for.

I told her we should really get club T-shirts. After all, there's got to be some perks to having a disability aside from kick ass parking. We began to figure out what names we should each put on our T-shirts. We had to have some outward representation of our challenges and identities so our fellow club members could find us. We decided on "Migraine Bi" for our bisexual friend and another was "Blind-something." As for mine, I haven't decided between

Fibro Jew or Fibro Degenerate for my Degenerative Disc Disease. But when we got to her, we struggled to figure out what her T-shirt name should be because there really isn't a ring to "Gastro Paresis or Ehlers Danlos Syndrome."

We're laughing and having a grand ol' time and her boyfriend starts feeling left out. He said he wanted a T-shirt name and that his should be something like "Immigrant working on type 2 diabetes" and I was like, "NO, you don't get a T-shirt name, you're not disabled, you haven't EARNED it!" And we all burst out in laughter and carried on with conversation. When her boyfriend had to leave, my friend explained how seizures were a potential side effect of the new medication she was on. And that's when it hit me! I said "OH, OH! THAT'S IT! Your T-shirt name is 'Shaky Puker!'"

And I think that's why we come to church. In the midst of big scaries, times of struggle and uncertainty, we seek connection and community. We look for comfort and humor from people who love us and hope to find others who understand the invisible pain we carry.

Puzzle Piece

I think I'm a difficult puzzle piece to fit. I'm about to be 26- which is fine with me because since I can remember, I felt like my age was catching up to who I've always been on the inside. However, the problem with being 26 and having a desire to find a partner to start growing the next part of your life is you come into the relationship with a lot of history and baggage. Only the lucky few find their forever person at a young age. A lot of people find a temporary person, mistaking them for their forever person, and they go through the things that give them baggage together until they either grow or separate.

When you go through difficult things with another person, it bonds you together forever. My parents, my sister, old high school friends, coworkers. Even the people you wish you weren't bonded to become that way anyway, such as past romantic relationships. I think this is the reason it feels so good to reconnect with someone from your history in which you have shared experiences. People seek closure from those who have left them with baggage to hold onto after they separated.

You see, when I went to the baggage claim of my soul, I used to keep it all very close to me, letting it pile up and take over. I offered to carry other people's baggage even when I ran out of arms and fingertips. I allowed myself to take their baggage with me, kicking it forward with my feet. It took me so much longer to get to where I was going, carrying around all this extra burden, that sometimes I missed my flight. At times, I'd put my own destination on hold because I'd have to catch a next nearest flight, getting layover after layover, until I forgot where I was supposed to be in the first place.

I think I'm an oddly shaped puzzle piece because when I finally had the courage to reach out a hand asking for assistance, they helped pull off the baggage I'd been carrying around for 20 years. Each ripping away parts of me that needed to be let go. I still find myself sorting through all my baggage to figure out what is mine and what is others. What parts of those trips to all those unexpected places do I want to keep and what is no longer necessary for me to hold on to? I suppose everyone does this at some point or another, or perhaps they must repeat this process over and over throughout their life. But when you're about to be 26 and you have enough trauma and lessons learned for a lifetime, it's difficult and lonely to find a puzzle piece that matches with yours.

Procedure Day

Toilet seats and I have a love/hate relationship. The obvious relief aside- if I sit on that thang for too long, my feet start to get tingly, my ass turns as red as an Irishman with a sunburn, and my hips and glutes feel like they're on fire. Tonight, as I sit on my toilet, typing away with my fingertips, my body aches and I have awful radiating pain going down from my low back, into my hips, glutes, down the sides of my thighs, to just behind my knees. Today I had my epidural procedure at the pain management doctor's office. It was my second time getting this procedure done and I walked in feeling much better than I did my first go-around.

The first time I had been predominately bed ridden for three weeks leading up to procedure day and was living in my own personal tormented hell- having recently discovered I have two degenerative spinal conditions amidst a global pandemic. Help has been minimal considering the circumstances. My loved ones are far away, and I've never felt the depth of such isolation. I could feel my fleeting sanity furthering itself from my mind a little more each passing day.

But this procedure day was going to be different. THIS TIME I knew what to expect. THIS TIME my body was stronger, and my mind was more prepared. Earlier in the day, I had physical therapy. I cooked some yummy food so I wouldn't have to post-procedure. I had a plan of action for loved ones to help me stay mentally present by being there virtually in case my PTSD got the better of me again. But alas, even with all the preparation and planning that time allowed, my PTSD still got the better of me and I was fighting my mind to keep from transporting back in time, reliving the movie reel of traumatic events throughout my life. The poor nurses who were tasked with prepping me for the procedure struggled to calm me and successfully get my IV started. It took three rounds to get that sucker in my arm. My veins like to run away from needles just as much as I do. Thankfully the staff were wonderful and when I got home I, for a little while, felt shocking okay.

The anxiety and panic that ravaged my body had subsided, and the pain wasn't terribly unbearable. Nevertheless, it didn't take very long for the feeling of hope for a chance at a pain free day to quickly fade- because THIS TIME really didn't turn out to be so different after all.

Pain flooded back in, overwhelming my senses as soon as the numbing agent the doctor used wore off. Fire as hot as those in California erupted in my hips and radiated down into my legs. Pain so intense my stomach began to churn and my head throbbed from all the tears I cried. In an effort to seek comfort, I video chatted with my dad and stepmom but seeing my father's face as he saw his little girl weep miles apart from him added a different kind of hurt that was similarly hard to bear.

Together we called the on-call doctor line from the pain management office to see if they would have any suggestions on how to ease my suffering and help me to make it through the night. The operator sent a message for whoever was on-call to return my plea for some much-needed assistance.

Fifty-seven minutes later, or an eternity (as it felt), I got a return call from a clearly inconvenienced doctor- as her tone and general demeanor made it known to me. She asked me to list what pain medication I have access to. To which I responded, bearing through the pain, with an account of the laundry list of meds I have nearby. Hearing the difficulty I was having getting through my words, she asked in a harsh tone, "Why are you talking like that?" To which I responded, probably (definitely), with more defensiveness than perhaps was warranted. I said, "Because I'm in pain and it's taking everything in me not to start crying again."

She asked if I had taken any medication. I said I hadn't because I wanted to get advice from a doctor before I did. She said, "Well you're supposed to take your regular medications even after having the procedure." I told her I did take my regular medication and responded what I meant was that I didn't take anything extra- reiterating I wanted to hear from a doctor first. She cut me off and said "Well you know, I can't prescribe you any medications."

I responded in my head first. *Jesus Christ, I know! I'm not drug seeking, lady!* Out loud I said sternly, and with decreasing patience, "I understand. I'm not asking you to. I'm asking for you to help me figure out what I can take out of the meds I have access to in my home, to help me deal with the pain."

She said "Oh. You have access to all of those medications at home?" I became frustrated because I felt like she had heard the words I stated but wasn't really listening to me.

In my head, *Yes! Didn't you hear me list off all the medications I have after you asked me to? How do you not listen to the answer to a question YOU asked ME moments ago?*

Out loud, "Yes, for the love of God." Whoops that one slip right out. Oh well. My usual threshold for niceties had long surpassed.

She told me which medication I could take out of the ones I had and advised me to put ice or heat on the affected area. "If that doesn't work," she said, "go to the emergency room." But the hospital is a far more dangerous place these days than the sting of this cold porcelain and tiled floor. I thanked her for the help and hung up quickly because I was done and had zero bandwidth to continue to talk to someone who didn't believe me or my "motives" in asking for help.

I did as was recommended and discovered that moving, surprisingly, made the pain a little better. Moving my legs around almost felt like doing my physical therapy exercises. So after meds and heat, I resorted to mildly shaking my legs back and forth. This was enough of a distraction for my brain that it short circuited and couldn't concentrate on both those movements and the pain at the same time- leading me to the decision to go for a walk outside. Probably (definitely) not the ideal thing to do. But it's me and I'm stubborn and unrelenting.

So, there I was- hobbling around in circles in the parking lot of my townhouse complex looking like an escaped patient from a hospital ward pushing an empty wheelchair. Using it as a walker to decrease my risk of falling. Thank God it was two in the morning. I would have, for sure, scared the daylights out of some children if I had been seen. Can you imagine seeing that outside your window during a pandemic? Yikes.

Pain is a funny thing. As a person who is privileged enough to live with an invisible disability, where I can still work and pass as able-bodied most of the time, I often forget or take for granted the simple pleasures of good parking spots, mostly level sidewalks, and walkable distances. After exhausting myself doing my crazy lady laps, I put my wheelchair back in my car and immediately had to sit on the ground before making the remarkably short walk from the car to my front door.

While sitting on the ground, twigs on ass, I thought back to the time I debated whether or not to get a handicap parking spot outside my house. The parking lot was mere yards away from the door. I figured even if I didn't get my desired spot, the other side to the parking lot only added a few more steps. But there I was, parked in my very close handicap spot, staring at my front door, feeling like I had the length of the great wall of China ahead of me. Pain can make the nearest goal that isn't too far out of reach feel so impossible.

Finally, back inside, sitting on my toilet winded from my adventure in the wilderness of my suburban cul-de-sac, I feel the pain rush back in- reminding me it never really left in the first place. Getting myself up the stairs after that walk was no small feat. As I sit on this cold porcelain, I feel all the nerves in my lower extremities catch ablaze. I find myself wondering if relief will ever come.

The Class of 2012

For some of us, high school was the pinnacle of our lives. It's where we mastered our domain, and we met our best friends. For others it was the place we swore we'd never go back to. Or if we did, our glow up would be so magnificent our very presence would prove those that tore us down they were wrong. But we are so much more than a group of people who happened to coexist around one another sharing a youthful experience. As different as we may be, we all share in common a place in time.

This school
This town

And I would argue that if we have that much in common, there's bound to be so much more just below the surface. So, get to know each other again, or introduce yourself for the first time. Find out what adventures life has taken us on in the years since we've been together. There is so much we have to be proud of. We are a community bonded by memories, choices, achievements, mistakes. And we have a responsibility to one another. To be there when one of us calls. To lift up those still finding their way. We are each other's past but we are also the future.

We are world travelers
Authors
Artists
We are GED graduates
Degree seekers and degree keepers
We are human beings overcoming addiction
Depression
Waking up every day if for no other reason than to prove to our high school selves we are STILL here
WE made it
Not all of us have
And tonight we honor those we've lost by being here, together
We are mothers, fathers, and parents raising the future tomorrow brings
We are doctors
Nurses
Social workers coming to aid the community we serve
We are plumbers
Teachers
Postal service workers
Graveyard shift- working til the sun comes up-ers
We are dreamers
Believers
We are the class of 2012

The Unspoken

I find it curious the amount of people who live to tell only a fraction of their story. Human beings are like walking universes. Each complex and unique, far more alike than different yet still resembling icebergs in their authenticity- so much more laying just below the surface. I have always prided myself on being an open person. However, the struggles I've had with my mental health are something, I'm sad to say, I find too embarrassing to speak on much of the time. I much prefer to share the silver linings, the humor in unfortunate mishaps, and the grand triumphs over the obstacles that have separated me from my ambitions.

I've never truly hated anyone or anything in my life but what comes close is my detest for being seen as weak or fragile. This is not a story that many, until now, will have heard. It is one in which I've internally debated whether or not to share- as if pacing back and forth in my mind. I've come to the conclusion that keeping it locked away for only few to witness has done me more harm than good over the years. Much like I have experienced with my creative writing and poetry, storytelling tragic moments in a humorous way has helped release me from the clutches of darkness, time and time again.

When I was 16, I tried to take my own life. I do not wish to comment more on that other than to say I am so glad I did not succeed. Despite my mental illness trying to convince me otherwise, I have amounted to so much more than I ever could have imagined. I am a world traveler, a crusader for social justice, and a helper to he communities in which I find myself part of, both personally and professionally. I help broken and forgotten people, just like me, every day. I am proud to say I now fully believe the world is a better place with me in it. But that's not what this story is about. This story is about a nasty shrew named Linda. Clearly, I'm not a card carrying member of the nurse Linda fan club and this story will explain why.

After I tried to take my own life, I found myself on an uncomfortable bed, in a small room, with terrible wallpaper, and even worse lighting. There was a single florescent light that imitated a window looking out to the sky- which when you have a lot of medication in your system is really quite amusing. Clouds billowed in that little room with the perfectly square foot of light cracked open, peaking toward that sky of make-believe. After leaving that room with the nice ladies who asked all sorts of questions, I was sent to an inpatient mental health hospital where I stayed for about two months. Because I had a lot of medical problems, I was able to explain my extended absence to my classmates as "being in the hospital" and no one really had any follow up questions. That was a super cool, albeit unexpected, perk to living with chronic illness.

The hospital ward wasn't like what you see in the movies. There were colorful carpets, doctors' offices, classrooms, and communal areas with games and fun activities. The food was good, and the people were generally nice and eager to help you. That is, except for nurse Linda. My practical self might see that she was a good person trying to do good deeds for the patients she cared for. But while I choose to believe that is likely true, I also allow myself to have anger and hurt at the pain she caused me. Even good people, doing good deeds, can still create an environment that fosters fear and wields power inappropriately.

Linda looked like her name. A woman of average height and build with short white hair that framed her face nicely. With pasty ivory skin that had started to thin and wrinkle at the edges of her eyes and neck. She had dark-framed glasses that sat toward the tip of her nose when she examined the charts and med lists on her silver clipboard- peering out at the room she occupied, calling out names one by one with a sharp rigid tone. Linda commanded her domain. Perhaps the only place she felt powerful.

Each day felt like forever, but the weeks went by quickly- somehow forgetting all the time that passed since I last felt freedom. But at least I was safe from myself, and that's all that mattered. It's a strange feeling to be grateful to a place that holds some of your greatest tragedies. Without it, I might not be here to tell this story- as a published author, no less. But still the memories of that place haunt me enough to still provoke fear at every doctor's appointment and distrust most medical providers, sight unseen.

The children's floor, where patients resided, was a long corridor with rooms on either side of the hallway. In the middle was a common area that held a small meeting lounge and the med room where Linda spent most of her time. There was a laundry room, another shared space at the end of one wing, and several large bathrooms with standing showers. Where, if you were deemed too much a threat to yourself, you got to enjoy supervised dumps- being sure to carefully avoid eye contact. At

the time I was admitted to the hospital, my chronic pain symptoms had remained undiagnosed. I was a medical mystery for seven years before I was diagnosed with Fibromyalgia. A normal, healthy-looking, child on the outside with hot searing pain that radiates throughout my body on the inside.

Doctors from all over the state had performed medical tests, experimented with treatments, medicated me with narcotics and steroids, all in search of an answer to the question "What's wrong with me?" It was after six years without a diagnosis that I tried to take my life, never fully realizing, until adulthood, how much of an impact my medical challenges had on my sanity. As a result of going so long without an answer, coupled with being an otherwise normal-appearing kid, it was pretty common for people to not believe the invisible pain that held me captive. Linda was one of many who doubted the pain I felt. As I was trapped in a body that held my spirit back from realizing its full potential, in a world that told me I was crazy, dramatic, and attention-seeking when I couldn't hold back my tears. I learned that keeping my pain to myself was the safest place for it to be. A dangerous lesson for a child to learn.

One day, I awoke to the morning announcement that it was time to get up and start our daily routine. Brush teeth, take meds, get dressed, rinse, repeat. But that morning was different. I could feel the muscles of my back and legs tighten, as if rebelling against my brain who was instructing them to move. I ached severely and asked one of the aides if they could bring me my medication from the med room. A request I didn't think was too much to ask. Linda, however, felt differently. She sent the aide back to me with instructions to get them myself or I wouldn't get them at all. I tried to explain why I was asking for help in getting them- moving hurt. Ping-ponging the aide, once again, back to nurse Linda. Before they could even return with the same message of refusal, I had already started to cramp up and spasm in one of my legs and shoulder blades- yelping out in pain. But Linda, fervent in her direction, did not believe the truth of my pain, and once again, refused to help me by bringing the medication that would've stopped the fire erupting in my body.

I laid there begging the aides to help me. Maybe if they had just explained a little better that I wasn't trying to be bad, Linda would see I was a good girl who just needed help to get my medication on that particular morning. The pain intensified. I started to squirm, and my arms began vigorously shaking back and forth as if I were having a seizure. This wasn't unusual for me. These episodes were growing in frequency at home and at school before I had stepped foot into that place. Flashes of ambulance rides, doctors with large metallic needles, the sounds of me wailing against school bells alerting students to stay in their classrooms all flooded my mind as I laid there wanting to die.

Why would anyone make this up for attention? Why did Linda want to punish me? The pain became too great, and my stomach started to churn, upheaving bile from my empty stomach. I cried out for help, laying in a pool of my own vomit, begging for Linda to step down from her power trip long enough to see I wasn't faking. Unmoving, she refused. She instructed one of the aides to keep an eye on me and make sure I did as she ordered. I wanted to prove to her I wasn't trying to be bad. I really did want to follow her instructions. I attempted to move from my bed, but my arms and legs weren't strong enough to hold me up off the ground. I fell onto that hard charcoal-colored carpet, counting the flecks of dust in front of my face. I vomited once more. Unable to escape the feeling of drowning in my own fluids. It felt like hours before Linda finally appeared to find me on the ground, sobbing. She picked up my torso in her arms, feeling the muscles in my back spasm for the first time- evidence that proved my innocence. Her eyes widened realizing what she had done.

"Relax your muscles, Jen." She repeated over and over. I can still hear the froggy pitch of her voice inside my head.

Gee Linda, maybe if you brought me the muscle relaxer medication I was prescribed, I would be able to fulfill that request.

It's all a bit of a blur after that. It felt as if my mind had left my body. Linda left me on the floor, silenced like stone, exhausted from crying. I suspect one of the aides who really liked me, who previously left the room unable to continue to watch my continuous suffering, called for some back up. Appearing like an angel, a beautiful, blonde-haired, woman came into my room to find me on the ground, soaked in tears and vomit.

"Help. Please, help me," I managed to whisper out.

And just like that she called out demanding an explanation for what she walked in on. It must have looked like a horror show, judging from the look on her face. That's certainly how it felt. She quickly yelled for someone to bring me my medication.

This story doesn't really have a happy ending. I don't

remember much about that day after that incident. I do remember, however, that Linda started bringing me prayer cards every day after that until I was eventually discharged. Was that her way of apologizing? I guess I'll never know. All I know is it felt like she was weaponizing her religion against me. To me, it seemed to say only Jesus can save me- not the medication created to treat my symptoms. My tears weren't holy-enough water to cast my demons out of me, so maybe these handy dandy cards will do the trick.

While I remind myself that Linda is just another human being walking through the world doing the best she can, it's okay to give myself permission to not like her and not respect her or her actions that cost me dearly. I hope whatever God she prayed to forgave her because I sure didn't for a very long time. Forgiveness doesn't take away from your experience of a person. It only allows you to let go of the hurt and anger that prevents you from moving forward with your life after that experience is over.

Hand-Me-Down Legacy

My grandfather lived in a world where monsters walked the earth. The monsters lived across the world in a distant land. And even though his family fled the land in time to escape the monsters' grasp- crossed oceans, hiked tall mountains, hid in vast grassy plains- he could still feel the echoes of fear and death left in the monsters wake.

As a little boy, he learned to arm himself with weaponry to fight them. As he grew, so did his bravery. He was valiant- a strength unmatched by any I have ever known. And as the years went on, the monsters weakened, war faded, and human beings were left counting their loved ones, for not everyone made it. It had seemed as though the monsters had been defeated.

My grandfather soon married a beautiful, kind hearted woman, who brought light and life back into his eyes. Together they built a castle on top of a hill and filled it with children and grandchildren, like me. They talked loudly, laughed loudly, loved loudly. And as the years went on, my grandfather knew peace.

However, the monsters were more difficult to defeat than we thought. They were masters of disguise- masking themselves and their true intentions. And just like wind is hard to see, so too was the fear and hate that lived in their hearts and minds.

My grandfather was older and unable to fight as he once had. He took my hand, kissed me on my keppela, and gathered the rest of his grandchildren and led them out of the castle, down the hill to a row boat on the shore of a lake. The water glistened as the sun began to rise.

We rowed to the middle of the lake, taking turns with the oars, as my grandfather was shaking and solemn. It was quiet. Only the sound of the boat slowly pushing through the water could be heard. We arrived at a dock, anchored to a large chain. My grandfather reached below the water pulling out a smaller chain and slowly pulling whatever it was holding out of the darkened blue depths. He cleared his throat.

"I have something for you all," he said. "I was hoping you would never need it."

A large trunk emerged from the water. The grandchildren gasped and looked at each other. Inscribed on the trunk were the words-

פֿאַר די טויט און די לעבעדיק מיר מוזן עדות זאָגן
far di toyt aun di lebedik mir muzn edus zogn.
Meaning, "For the dead and the living, we must bear witness."

My grandfather reached in his pocket, pulling out a key to the trunk, his hands shaking as he reached to unlock it. My eldest cousin placed his hand on my grandfather's and said, "It's okay, grandpa, I can do it." My eldest cousin inserted the key into the rusted lock and turned it with great effort. After a few seconds of struggling, the key clicked into place, releasing the clasp. Tears fell gently onto my grandfather's cheeks.

The grandchildren recognized the black insignia on a red cloth as the markings on the monsters they had seen in history books. There were old books with scuffs and tears on their binding, gold teeth, and photos of skeletal-looking people with numbers tattooed on their forearms. The grandchildren also found damaged clothing, several pairs of small shoes, crumpled papers with large noses and angry eyes in newspaper cutouts from years long past in a language the grandchildren didn't recognize.

As the grandchildren continued to look through the different items in the trunk, they looked up at my grandfather with confusion and curiosity in their eyes.

My youngest cousin asked, "I don't understand, what's so special about this stuff?"

My grandfather cleared his throat and said this trunk contained all of the weapons he used to fight off the monsters. He explained that the monsters were never large scary creatures, but rather other human beings who collectively used their hate and fear to dictate their treatment of those who were different from them. As their hate and ignorance grew, the worse they treated those around them, nearly destroying the world in the process.

My grandfather looked at us grandchildren, one by one, and said the reason he kept his collection of weapons was so he could retell the history of our people, to honor the memory of those who perished in war, and to strengthen the bond our family has to our heritage.

"It is my wish for you to take these books, papers, photos, and clothing and use them to educate yourselves and those around you," my grandfather said. He went on, "It is my hope you will go on to help unite the world, celebrate the differences of others, and treat everyone with dignity and compassion.

"It is important to recognize and acknowledge the humanity in hatred and fear. We cannot truly progress or change the world for the better if we continue to separate the past from the present; to say what once was, is no more. It is easy to distinguish a group of people as evil or monstrous in their actions and behavior, but it is much harder to accept that cruelty to such a high degree still prevails in our world today and will continue if we don't actively fight against it. Go on, grow and flourish. Lift up those around you and speak out against injustice. Find peace in your soul, take pride in your heritage, and carry on the legacy of our family."

On their journey back to the castle, the rowboat made it's way through the water. The sun had fully risen, giving life to a new day, and the hope of a new beginning.

ABOUT THE AUTHOR

JENNA COHEN

Miss Cohen is a social worker, activist and organizer, public speaker, and spray paint artist. *Time Well Spent*, a collection of poetry, songs, and short essays is Cohen's publishing debut.

Miss Cohen is originally from upstate New York, where she graduated, Class of 2012, from the Rod Serling School of Fine Arts within Binghamton High School. While Miss Cohen started writing music and poetry when she was five years old, she credits the development of her artistic skills to her high school art and music teachers. Miss Cohen uses her art and community outreach work to aid her and others in their healing, spread awareness, and fight for equity and equality everywhere.

Acknowledgments

To my parents, for always encouraging me to be myself and to pursue my passions. To my grandfather who has always inspired me to take care of myself and the world around me. I would like to thank my village for helping to raise me to be the woman I proudly am today.

My Village:

- My entire family
- Summerhill family
- Thorpe Family
- Taylor Family
- McCoy-Tabachnick Family
- Poplawski Family
- Wenig Family
- Unitarian Universalist Congregation of Binghamton
- Binghamton High School
- Mrs. Waples
- Ms. Sickler
- Camp Sertoma

Made in United States
North Haven, CT
11 December 2022

28422942R00049